195

Walter Trobisch
My wife Made Me a Polygamist

Walter Trobisch

My Wife Made
Me a Polygamist

(New revised and completed edition)

INTER-VARSITY PRESS
Downers Grove, Illinois 60515

Books of EDITIONS TROBISCH can be ordered in the United States through INTER-VARSITY PRESS, Downers Grove, Illinois, 60515; in Canada through Inter-Varsity Book Room, 745 Mount Pleasant Road, Toronto 298, Ontario.

Have you read the other books in this series?

Love Is a Feeling to Be Learned
My Parents Are Impossible
Please Help Me! Please Love Me!
Better Is Your Love Than Wine

USA ISBN 0-87784-436-4

Gesamtherstellung:
St.-Johannis-Druckerei C. Schweickhardt, Lahr 2, (Germany)
11496/1971

FOREWORD

Originally this book was meant as a textbook for teaching family-life seminars in Africa. However, the high divorce rate indicates that the problem of "successive polygamy" as well as that of the "triangle marriage" is also a vital one in so-called monogamous societies of America and Europe — and wherever western influence spreads. Therefore this book is made available now to a wider reading public.

As far as Africa is concerned, recent publications by church leaders and missionaries show a growing insight into the fact that the disciplinarian approach to the problem of polygamy has failed. The counseling approach to husbands and wives living in polygamous marriage as proposed in this book is new. We are still here in the experimental stage. Therefore I welcome constructive criticism, especially from those who live in polygamous marriages — be it an African or western type — and from those who care for such people.

Walter Trobisch
Lichtenberg 6
A-4880 St. Georgen i. A.
Austria

On one of my trips I worshipped in an African church where nobody knew me. After the service I talked to two boys who had also attended.

"How many brothers and sisters do you have?" I asked the first one.

"Three."

"Are they all from the same stomach?"[1]

"Yes, my father is a Christian."

"How about you?" I addressed the other boy.

He hesitated. In his mind he was adding up the number of children. I knew immediately that he came from a polygamous family.

"We are nine," he finally said.

"Is your father a Christian?"

"No," was the typical answer, "he is a polygamist."

"Are you baptized?"

"Yes, and my brothers and sisters too," he added proudly.

"And their mothers?"

1 Literal translation from the African language meaning that they have the same mother.

"They are all three baptized, but only the first wife takes communion."

"Take me to your father."

The boy led me to a compound with many individual houses. It breathed an atmosphere of cleanliness, order and wealth. Each wife had her own house and her own kitchen. The father, a middle-aged, good-looking man, tall, fat and impressive, received me without embarrassment and with apparent joy.

I found Omodo to be a well-educated man, wide awake and intelligent, with a sharp wit and a rare sense of humor. In the following dialog I will attempt to restate the gist of our long conversation. From the outset he made no apologies about being a polygamist.

"Welcome to the hut of a poor sinner." The words were accompanied by hearty laughter.

"It looks like a rich sinner," I retorted.

"The saints very seldom come to this place," he said. "They don't want to be contaminated with sin."

"But they are not afraid to receive your wives and children. I just met them in church."

"I know. I give everyone a coin for the collection plate. I guess I finance half of the church's budget. They are glad to take my money, but they don't want me."

I sat in thoughtful silence. After a while he continued.

"I feel sorry for the pastor. By refusing to accept all the polygamous men in town as church members he has made his flock poor and they shall always be dependent upon subsidies from America. He has created a church of women whom he tells every Sunday that polygamy[2] is wrong."

"Wasn't your first wife heartbroken when you took a second one?"

Omodo looked at me almost with pity.

"It was her happiest day," he said.

"Tell me how it happened."

"Well, one day after she had come home from the garden and had fetched wood and water, she was preparing the evening meal while I sat in front of my house and watched her. Suddenly she turned to me and mocked me. She called me a poor man, because I only had one wife. She pointed to our neighbor's wife who could care for her children while the other wife prepared the food."

"'Poor man!'" Omodo repeated. "I can take a lot, but not that. And I had to admit she was

2 Polygamy is used in this book in the sense of poly-gyny (the marriage of one man with more than one wife). In Africa it is used mostly in this sense because polyandry (the marriage of one woman with more than one husband) is unknown.

right. She needed help. She had already picked out a second wife for me. They get along fine."

I glanced around the courtyard and saw a beautiful young woman, about 19 or 20, come out of one of the huts.

"It was a sacrifice for me," Omodo commented. "Her father demanded a very high *lobola* (bridewealth)."

"Do you mean that the wife who caused you to become a polygamist is the only one of your family who receives communion?"

"Yes, according to the church my wives are considered obedient to God's will regarding marriage because each of them has only one husband. I, the husband and father, am the only sinner in our family. The Lord's Supper is given to sinners, but I am excluded from it. Can you understand that, pastor?"

I was confused.

"And you see," Omodo continued, "they are all praying for me that I might be saved from sin, but they don't agree from which sin I must be saved."

"What do you mean?"

"Well, the pastor prays that I may not continue to commit the sin of polygamy. My wives pray that I may not commit the sin of divorce. I wonder whose prayers are heard first."

"So your wives are afraid that you will become a Christian?"

"They are afraid that I will become a church member. Let's put it that way. For me there is a difference. You see they can only have intimate relations with me as long as I do not belong to the church. The moment I become a church member, their marriage relations with me become sinful."

"Wouldn't you like to become a church member?"

"Pastor, don't lead me into temptation. How can I become a church member if it means to disobey Christ? Christ forbade divorce, but not polygamy. The church forbids polygamy, but demands divorce. How can I become a church member if I want to be a Christian? For me there is only one way — to be a Christian without the church."

"Have you ever talked to your pastor about that?"

"He does not dare to talk to me because he knows as well as I do that some of his elders have a second wife secretly. The only difference between them and me is that I am honest and they are hypocrites."

"Did a missionary ever talk to you?"

"Yes, once. I told him that Europe and America have a successive form of polygamy — divorce — while we have a simultaneous polygamy. Ours is more honest, more humane. That did it. He never came back."

I decided to remain silent and asked Omodo to accompany me back to the village. He gladly obliged. Evidently he enjoyed being seen with a pastor.

"But tell me, why did you take a third wife?" I asked him while we were walking.

"I did not take her. I inherited her and her children from my late brother. Actually my older brother would have been next in line. But he is a church elder and not allowed to sin by giving security to a widow."

I looked in his eyes. "Do you want to become a Christian?"

"I *am* a Christian," he said without smiling.

My silent response to Omodo did not mean that I agreed with everything he said. But I wanted him to feel that I accepted him as he was, not that I judged him without knowing his situation. Therefore, instead of arguing, I decided to listen. My experience has been that if I listen long enough, most people point themselves toward the help they need.

Listening is harder than speaking. It is much more tiresome. Listening to Omodo and making a real effort to understand him before judging him demanded concentration, empathy and the willingness to see things within a framework different from my own.

But when Omodo, without smiling, made his confession of faith at the end of our conversation, I knew that a bond was established between us. It was as if he extended an invitation to me to continue our talk.

I regret that I was not able to see Omodo again. But I have thought much about him and others in similar situations. While I was talking to Omodo, a word which Jesus had said to the Pharisees kept coming to my mind: "You blind guides, straining out a gnat and swallowing a camel!" (Mt. 23 : 24).

It is always healthy to see one's self with someone else's eyes. So the first question I asked myself was, "Where is Omodo right?"

Basically, he makes two accusations: First, that the policies practiced by churches and missions in Africa in dealing with the problem of polygamy are illogical, contradictory and arbitrary, and second, that the church's and mission's stand against polygamy is contradictory to the Bible.

There can be no doubt that Omodo is right in his first accusation. Most of today's African church leaders and many missionaries would admit that.

Rev. Judah B. M. Kiwovele, President of the Southern Synod of the Evangelical Lutheran Church in Tanzania says: "The answers given by leaders of the Church and missions as defenders

13

of monogamy do not satisfy. . . . There is a request to reconsider both missionary methods and Church structure."[3]

The picture is indeed confusing. Some churches demand that a polygamous man separate from all his wives; others demand that he separate from all but one. But there is disagreement about which one. Some say that he must keep his first wife; others allow him to choose for the sake of the smaller children. None of the churches has come forth with a satisfactory answer to what should happen to the wives who are sent away — who, after all, were married and had their husband's promise of lifelong responsibility for them and their children. (This is the meaning of "lobola" which Omodo mentions.)

Some churches permit these wives to stay with their husband under the condition that he has no sexual relations with them. Evidently they see the "sinfulness" of polygamy mainly in the performance of the sex act.

Strangely enough, as far as church membership goes, most churches take issue only with the man, not — as Omodo rightly observed — with the women. Usually all of the wives are baptized, although sometimes it is only the first wife who is permitted to take Holy Communion. But no one has been able to explain just which interpretation of the sacraments justifies this practice.

3 AFRICAN THEOLOGICAL JOURNAL, February 1969.

Some churches do not even allow polygamist husbands to enter catechumen class. Others allow them to do so, but do not baptize them. Again others baptize them, but exclude them from the Lord's Supper. A few, for example, the Lutheran Church of Liberia, allow polygamist husbands full church membership. But even they do it only under two conditions: that he "entered into polygamous union in ignorance of the Christian Gospel and Law" and that he not "hold office in the Church or congregation or be engaged as a Christian worker."[4]

In short, the contradictions are so evident that it is no use to even argue this point with Omodo. The policies are not only contradictory in themselves, but, worst of all, the churches contradict their teachings by their practice. Rev. Kiwovele says: "If salvation were based on monogamous marriages . . . the salvation looks as though it were earned meritoriously, by fulfilling certain conditions rather than given by the grace of God through repentance of sins and faith in Jesus as Saviour of mankind." Rev. Adejunmobi from the Baptist Church in Nigeria adds: "What the Independent African Churches question is the making of a right marriage a passport to salvation, or at least to church membership."

This contradiction between doctrine and practice did not escape Omodo either, when he observed, in a slighted manner, "I, the husband

4 Minutes of the Third Biennial Convention, Zorzor, Liberia, January 1951.

and father, am the only sinner in our family. The Lord's Supper is given to sinners, but I am excluded from it."

There's no point in arguing with Omodo here. He is right. The African churches face a problem here which simply has not yet been solved. The picture on the African scene is one of uttermost helplessness. One must admit too that the disciplinary approach — I could also call it the "church-membership approach" — has entirely failed.

Rev. Joseph Conrad Wold, a Lutheran missionary in Liberia, says:

Missionaries become hair-splitting legalists like the Pharisees, willing to cross seas and mountains to make a single convert, and then lay on them burdens that they themselves are not called upon to bear. For the pagan the distinction is apt to be, not between those who follow Christ and those who do not, but between those who practice polygamy and those who do not. The missionaries have tried to reject polygamy by rejecting polygamists . . .

The grace of God will not be bound in the cultural box of Western social patterns. If uncircumcised Gentiles can receive the Holy Spirit and be baptized (Acts 10 : 44), then, by the grace of God, polygamists can become Christians without being forced to thrust a wife into adultery or break a serious and honorable promise to a wife's father and family . . . If man is lost, let it be because he refused to accept

Christ as risen Lord and Saviour, and not because he loved both his wives too much to disgrace and ruin them, or was too upright to lie, or live in deceit.[5]

How I wish that my friend Omodo — "too upright to lie or to live in deceit" — could read these lines! It would at least show him that he is not alone, that there are people who start to understand him.

I am grateful that, in Christ, we have the freedom to accept defeat. In him we are redeemed from the love of self-defense out of hurt pride. Accepting defeat and humiliation is certainly a better testimony to our crucified Saviour than futile arguments in order to "save face". I am sure that Omodo was greatly surprised that I accepted defeat. At the same time we both started to feel that we had something in common, that we started to broadcast at the same wave length.

Omodo, however, did not just attack church policy. He did much more. He played the church against the Bible, against Jesus Christ himself: "How can I become a church member if it means to disobey Christ? Christ forbade divorce, but not polygamy. The church forbids polygamy, but demands divorce."

In other words, Omodo accuses the church of having misinterpreted the Bible and of having disobeyed her Lord. Is he right here too? The

5 GOD'S IMPATIENCE IN LIBERIA (Grand Rapids: William B. Eerdmans, 1967), pp. 179 ff.

answer is much more difficult than the answer to his attack on church policies. For here the answer has to be *Yes* — and *No*.

At first glance he seems to be right. For the Old Testament writers, polygamy was indeed a legally recognized form of marriage and home life. Nowhere is it considered "permanent adultery", as I once heard a missionary say. Adultery is never permanent. It is a momentary relationship in secrecy with no responsibility involved.

In contrast "a polygamous marriage", says Rev. Gerhard Jasper, Tutor at the Lutheran Theological College, Makumira, Tanzania, "is, for the Old Testament, a marriage in the fullest sense of the word with all the protection which the law and the elders of Israel could give to it. An Israelite who had two wives was by no means considered one who had fallen in his faith or in the necessary obedience in faith. He was not placed into the category of a second-class Israelite who was under discipline and first had to repent before he would be admitted to full congregational membership."[6]

The difficulty is, however, that in the Old Testament polygamy receives a different rating depending upon which way of life it is compared with. Therefore the answer to Omodo's criticism has to be Yes and No.

Compared with the way of life of Israel's

6 AFRICAN THEOLOGICAL JOURNAL, February 1969, p. 41.

neighbors in Canaan, polygamy was still the better solution. There Israel witnessed a morass of lax sexual behavior. The worship of the Canaanitic gods of fertility involved intercourse with temple harlots and, since practically the line between cultic and secular harlotry was hard to draw, prostitution as such.

Therefore all extramarital relationships were as rigidly condemned in Israel as in many African tribal societies in the precolonial era. Adultery deserved capital punishment (Deut. 22 : 21; Lev. 20 : 10) and, to make this point clear, the term "adultery" included, in Israel, also premarital relations, since the whole conception of life was seen in view of the future marriage (Deut. 22 : 21).

Contrasted with such sexual licentiousness, polygamy was tolerated in Israel as by far the smaller evil. Sometimes grudgingly — one even has the impression that some of the writers of the Old Testament were embarrassed to report it — but it was tolerated.

However, it must be stated that marriage in Israel was generally monogamous. Adam, Isaac, Noah and the prophets Hosea and Isaiah should be mentioned as examples. Contrasted with monogamy the polygamous way of life fell under sharp criticism.

With relentless realism the Old Testament does not tire of pointing out the negative aspects of polygamy.

Abraham's polygamy is reported as a criticism.

No blessing rested upon it. It constituted a poor, human makeshift solution, a sign of lack of faith, leading to contempt, jealousy quarrelling in the home and estrangement between husband and wife (Gen. 16 and 21).

Esau's two wives "made life bitter" (Gen. 26 : 35) and Jacob had nothing but trouble with the two sisters he married within one week. There was rivalry and hatred in his home (Gen. 29 : 30-31), envy and wrestling between the two wives (Gen. 30 : 1, 8) and finally anger between him and even his favorite wife Rachel who was unhappy and desperate (Gen. 30 : 2).

Then the jealousy continued among the children. The story of Joseph, the son of Jacob's favorite wife Rachel (Gen. 37), cannot be understood without the warning message against polygamy which it contains. His brothers cannot "speak peaceably" to Joseph; they conspire to kill him and finally sell him into slavery.

In the story of Abimelech, polygamy actually leads to murder. In a war of succession, he kills his 69 brothers with the help of his maternal uncles (Judg. 9 : 5). The same is reported about King David. The features of the Jacob story repeat themselves — favoritism and injustice. His sons kill each other since their adulterous father has lost all authority to settle the question of heritage (2 Sam. 14). When finally through last minute intrigues, Solomon (the son of David's favorite wife, Bathsheba) became king (1 Kings 1), his kingdom too was ruined through polygamy for "his

wives turned away his heart after other gods"
(1 Kings 11 : 4).

This is a very dark picture indeed. For Africans,
however, it is not hard to believe. It confirms the
scepticism expressed by many African proverbs
and stories. This is the daily pageant of polygamous family life: heritage quarrels, succession
feuds, tribal wars, endless intrigues, murder or at
least the constant fear of being killed by magic
power used in the interest of the adversary. (In
Africa there is a direct link between black magic
and polygamy.)

Therefore, Omodo is not right when he indis-
criminately claims the Old Testament for the case
of polygamy. Confronted with the sexual morass
of Israel's neighbors, it may have been the smaller evil for the time being until deeper spiritual
insights could grow. Compared to monogamy, the
Bible has little to say in defense of polygamy. It
falls intolerably short of God's will for marriage.

The Old Testament leaves no doubt about God's
will here. In the creation story as recorded in
Genesis 2 the Bible sets forth, powerfully and
with indisputable clarity, monogamy as God's
original and final will. This story breathes the spirit
of monogamy in every word, line, illustration and
comparison.

God plans Adam's wife as "a helper fit for
him" (Gen. 2 : 18). This Hebrew expression means
an equal partner, a correcting opposite — not a
subordinate servant. Such equality is only pos-

21

sible in a monogamous union, for polygamy enhances the subordination of women.

The story of the creation of this helper out of one of Adam's ribs is only understandable as an illustration of monogamy: Since they are taken from the same material, the two parts fit together exactly again. The creation story conceives of the "one flesh union" in the first place as an anatomical completion, involving thus an exclusive relationship. This comparison is unthinkable within the context of a polygamous image of marriage. A third part would have no place in it.

This exclusive relationship extends then to all the other realms of life — material, emotional and spiritual — proposing marital love as an exclusive relationship, possible only between one man and one wife.

Though the word "love" is not mentioned, the whole story is actually an unmatched description of the reality of love, of monogamous love.

The idea is this: Because they are taken from the same material, the two equal parts are drawn together again with irresistible power, a power which can grow only between one husband and one wife, a power stronger than all family ties.

"Therefore (because of this power of love) *a man leaves his father and his mother and cleaves to his wife, and they become one flesh"* (Gen. 2 : 24).

With these words of inexhaustible depth and

divine wisdom, the biblical witness who speaks in Genesis 2 sums up the creation story, proclaiming a message which he believes valid for all times and all cultures. In his time this message contained an anti-polygamous spearhead, pointedly addressed to the corrupt government circles of Israel, corrupt through polygamy in the places of King David and King Solomon. It was proclaimed with the intention of bringing forth change in Israel.

And it did. It started a process, a movement.[7] It permeated the thinking of the nation. The Old Testament testifies to this process. More and more, monogamy emerges as the ideal form of marriage. During the time of the New Testament the message of Genesis 2 : 24 had brought forth change to such a degree that simultaneous polygamy seemingly was no longer a burning issue.

However, it was still practiced during the time of Jesus. His silence about this fact is, therefore, surprising. Could it mean that he was in favor of the counseling approach and rejected the disciplinarian approach?

In any case, the silence of the New Testament about polygamy is complete. The passage stipulating that a bishop or elder should be "hus-

7 This process of changing an institution by a message can be compared with the process by which the institution of slavery was overcome. Paul sent the slave Onesimus back to his master at the same time as he proclaimed a message incompatible with slavery. This message finally caused its downfall. But it took centuries.

band of one wife" (1 Tim. 3 : 1; Titus 1 : 5) may not even refer to polygamy, but rather advise against remarriage of a widowed church leader.

During the time of the New Testament, the issue had evidently changed from the issue of simultaneous polygamy to that of successive polygamy through easy divorce.

When Jesus was confronted with the question of divorce, he stood up against this successive form of polygamy by referring to the creation story: "Have you not read that he who made them from the beginning made them male and female, and said, 'For this reason a man shall leave his father and mother and be joined to his wife, and the two shall become one'? So they are no longer two but one. What therefore God has joined together let no one put asunder" (Matt. 19 : 4-6).

Then the Apostle Paul, comparing the love between husband and wife to love between Christ and the church, quoted Genesis 2 : 24, adding to it: "This is a great mystery, and I take it to mean Christ and the church" (Eph. 5 : 32). As a husband leaves his father and mother in order to cleave to his wife and become one flesh with her, Christ left his father, when he was born man (Phil. 2 : 7), his mother, when he died at the cross (John 19 : 26), and cleaves to his bride, the church, and becomes one with her as the one head to the one body (Eph. 1 : 22-23) in an exclusive relationship: "Husbands, love your wives, as Christ loved the church and gave himself up for her" (Eph. 5 : 25).

24

Thus the message of Genesis 2 : 24 became a key verse, the only verse about marriage quoted four times in the Bible. It started a dynamic process. This process is reflected in the Bible and is still going on in our day.

We are just now beginning to understand the full implications of this message. If monogamy means reflecting the love of Christ to his church, then monogamy is not a western concept of marriage pertaining only to one culture. It is a biblical concept, presenting a challenge to all cultures.

Certainly such togetherness as is proposed in Genesis 2 : 24 cannot grow in a polygamous home. Neither does the mere fact of being married to one spouse bring monogamy into realization in the deep sense in which the Apostle describes it. The exclusiveness as well as the full equality of the relationship between husband and wife is still highly disputed in the west and far from being realized. Sometimes it is my impression that the outwardly monogamous society of the west with its sex adoration, "free love", concubinage, prostitution, adultery and divorce may be further away from the biblical ideal and closer to the sexual morass of the Canaanitic fertility cults than the potentially polygamous society of Africa.

We are on our way together, Africans and westerners alike, involved in the same process. But it is not enough merely to work out a biblical ideal to refute Omodo's second accusation. It is not enough to admit, with Omodo, that the traditional approach of the church and missions is grossly inhumane and contradictory. Saying that one approach is wrong is not yet saying which approach is right. It is easy to tear down, but hard to build up. If the disciplinarian approach has failed, what is the alternative? To me there is only one: *We have to approach the problem through counseling.* By this method we help each other face the challenges of God's Word.

Two things have to be kept in mind.

First, both the polygamist and the monogamist participate in the same process. This should make the monogamist humble and help him avoid the "downward slant" in his attitude. But above all it should give him patience and make him careful not to ask more from the other one than he can put into practice, depending upon what stage of the process he is in.

Second, there are different motives leading to polygamy. For Abraham and Elkanah (1 Sam. 1) it was barrenness; for Lamech (Gen. 4 : 23) it was pride; for Gideon (Judg. 8 : 30) it was prestige; for Boaz, who married Ruth, the widow of one of his cousins (Ruth 4), it was the levirate marriage; for David and Solomon it was power and sexual lust.

The Bible discerns the motives. The disciplinary approach deals with polygamy as an object and tries to find a general approach. Therefore it has failed. The counseling approach deals with the polygamist. It is personal. It tries to match the answer to the motive.

Omodo's motive for taking a second wife was entirely different than his motive for taking a third. When talking to him again one would have to discern carefully his motives.

Omodo's first wife

Omodo's first wife was overburdened with work and wanted help. Therefore, she asked Omodo to become a polygamist. It is strange that missions and churches in Africa have almost entirely overlooked the female motive for polygamy. There is a justification for it. The African wife is overburdened. It is usually the man's work to clear the field of brush and trees, but she has to do all the other work — hoeing, planting, cultivating and harvesting.

To help here with this problem would not be easy and would take time. What is actually needed is momentous — to change the concept of marriage from a concept of inequality and subordination to a concept of partnership. The idea that garden work is women's work is not necessarily a correlate to a patriachal system. On the South Pacific Island of New Caledonia I found a patriarchal society with virtually no polygamy. The main reason was that the men helped their wives in the fields.

If I could have gone back to Omodo, I would have taken my wife along and asked her to tell him what she would think of me if I would let her work all day in the garden, get wood and water, care for the children and prepare the food, while I sat idly in the shade under the eaves of my hut and watched her work all day.

She would have explained to him what the Bible means, when the wife is called "a helper fit for him" (Gen. 2 : 18): an equal, a corresponding opposite, a partner. My wife might have told Omodo that he does not have three wives, but actually no wife at all. He is married to three female slaves. Consequently he is not a real husband, but just a married male. Only a real husband makes a wife a real wife. Since Omodo claimed that he was a Christian, he could not refuse this biblical challenge.

In the meantime, while my wife talked to Omodo, I would have talked to Omodo's first wife and told her precisely the same: Only a real wife makes a husband a real husband. She had not asked enough from her husband. She had behaved like an overburdened slave, trying to solve her problem by getting a second slave. Instead she should have asked her husband to help her. She should have behaved like a partner and expected partnership.

Neither Omodo nor his wife would have understood us immediately. It would have taken many talks, visit after visit, during weeks, months, maybe years. The disciplinary approach is the lazy approach. To count the number of wives and then to excommunicate the "guilty" man takes neither effort nor love. The counseling approach demands the hard work of love and patience.

After a while we would have talked to Omodo and his wife together, if at all possible. For this is the most effective way of marriage counseling — as a couple to couples. Unfortunately pastor's wives are usually not trained for this work and many pastors may not yet even have seen the possibilities here.

The only way to teach a marriage of partners is by example. One day we were discussing partnership in the marriage course I taught at Cameroun Christian College. The students were telling me that African women are just not yet mature enough to be treated as equal partners. While we were discussing this, it began to rain, pouring down on the metal roof. We watched through the window of the class room as an African teacher's wife jumped from her bicycle and sought refuge under the roof of the school building. After a little while a car drove up. Out stepped her husband, handed her the car keys (he must have taught her how to drive) and off she drove with the car, while he rode the bicycle, following her.

This settled the argument. It is the husband who makes his wife a partner, in monogamy as well.

Of course, one would have to investigate the concrete situation of Omodo and his wife in order not to demand too much at a time. They may desire to change, but not be able to do so immediately, especially if their gardens are so far apart that they cannot be taken care of by one person. However, this should not hinder at least challenging them toward this goal.

Omodo's second wife

It is interesting that barrenness of his first wife was not Omodo's motive for taking a second wife, as it was for Abraham and Elkanah and as it is very frequently in Africa today. Omodo's first wife had children and even sons.

Neither was his motive to space the births of his children. Polygamy in Africa has served as a method of "birth control", at least as seen from the point of view of the individual wife and mother. If these motives would have been involved, other advice would have to be given.[8]

Omodo said he took a second wife to give his first wife a helper: "It was her happiest day. . . . It was a great sacrifice for me."

When I saw the second wife, I had doubts. She was beautiful, but very young and fragile. She did not look as if she could do hard garden work, nor as if she had had much experience in the

8 In this case, the advice given in the book PLEASE HELP ME! PLEASE LOVE ME! would apply also to Omodo.

kitchen, let alone with children. Could it be that consciously or unconsciously there was a secondary motive involved here? That Omodo considered his first wife as "dark bread", while the second was to satisfy his appetite for sweets? I call this the "candy-motive", a motive which was certainly also involved in Jacob's marriage to Rachel.

I can well imagine the story of Omodo's "Rachel". She probably was given into marriage to Omodo at a very young age without her own consent. African fathers who are poor sometimes marry their young daughters to 60-year-old polygamists, because they are rich and can pay more. This is one of the dangers of the bride-wealth system.

The counseling approach would involve talking to Omodo's second wife and listening to her side of the story. It is significant that especially in the story of Jacob the Bible presents polygamy very pointedly also from the female aspect.

Young and attractive as Omodo's second wife was, it was hard to imagine that the affection was mutual. The age difference between her and old, fat Omodo must have been between 20 and 30 years. It is very likely therefore that she had a younger lover alongside.

Those who advise polygamy as an antidote against adultery see only part of the problem. Once an inclusive sex-partnership is accepted, the step toward adultery is easy to take. Women married to polygamous men often live individually in adultery because their husbands, staying usually with one wife for a week at a time or with the favorite wife only, are not able to satisfy them sexually. Again the story of Jacob hints toward this problem, when it reports that Leah had to "buy" her husband for one night from Rachel (Gen. 30 : 16).

It seems to me that the best way to solve the problem of Omodo's second wife would be to help her marry the man she loves. If she knew a man and wanted marriage, it would again involve hard work.

First, I would have to talk to Omodo, ask him to see her as a person with her own needs and inquire about his real motive in marrying her.

Then, I would have to talk to his first wife again and ask her how she feels now about this "helper". Does she feel jealous in her heart? Why did she choose her in the first place? Furthermore, why did she use the mocking technique ("poor man!") with her husband? Had she been hurt by something and taken revenge without really meaning it, while Omodo quickly jumped at the chance? All this would have to be carefully explored.

Next, I would talk to the young suitor of the second wife. Is he qualified? Is he fully aware of what he is doing? Would he accept a girl who is no longer a virgin? How about his own relationships to other girls?

Let us assume that these questions were satisfactorily answered and the second wife and young suitor decided to marry. This would involve talks with the family of Omodo's second wife and with the family of her future husband. Then the three families would have to talk and talk over the thorny question of bride-wealth. It would be quite a *palaver!* Omodo would have to be refunded and a new price settled for his former second wife, taking into account that she is now a divorced woman.

Is she? Yes. If polygamy is recognized as a legal form of marriage, polygamists cannot become monogamists without divorce. There is no solution to this dilemma. It can be justified only if both parties agree and if the divorced wife is cared for. If this is not the case or not possible, "it would be sheer brutality on the part of the Christian Church to confront men with the choice of baptism and institutional polygamy."[9]

But the talks we had up to this point would have enabled me to talk to Omodo meaningfully about sin. Not about the "sinfulness" of polygamy! That would be as of little avail as talking to a soldier about the sinfulness of war or to a slave about the sinfulness of slavery.

However, I could talk to him and his wives now about their concrete sins in their polygamous state — in the same way as I would talk to any monogamous couple with whom I wanted

9 Karl Barth, CHURCH DOGMATICS, III/4, p. 203.

to talk spiritually about their sins in their monogamous state.

So I would try to help Omodo to become honest about the "candy-motive", to see the selfishness of it and admit his lack of concern for his first overburdened wife and also of the second one, forced into marriage with him for his egotistic pleasure.

To Omodo's first wife I would have talked about her "happiest day", encouraging her to share the negative feelings against her husband which she was hiding in her heart und making her see the mistake of her mocking approach, by which she tore down his self-esteem as a man.

With the second wife I would have had a very serious talk about her adultery and also asked her why she had not become pregnant. Possibly she had used medicine to cause an abortion, a deed which deeply troubles the conscience of African women.

In this way the topic of our conversations would have switched from the topic of polygamy to the topic of "salvation given by the grace of God through repentance of sins and faith in Jesus as Saviour of mankind".

After Omodo had had a personal experience of forgiveness, I would have baptized him, even though we were still working on a solution for his second and third wife. I would have expected such a solution as a fruit of his baptism and not as a condition for it. As Pater Eugen Hillmann, a Roman Catholic missionary among the Masai people in Tanzania puts it: "A non-baptized person should not be expected to have actually attained the Christian ideal of marriage *before* he has had any possibility of participating in the sacramental life of the church."[10]

Omodo's third wife

The situation of Omodo's third wife is entirely different from the second. This fact illustrates again how important it is to discern the motives.

Her husband, Omodo's brother, had died. A widow is the most pitiful person in Africa. She is a property which has lost its proprietor. According to African custom, the brother of her late husband is responsible for her and her children — the same custom which in Israel was called the "levirate marriage". If she were to marry a man from another family, she would lose her children. The bride-wealth given for her by her late husband's clan included also the children. So she has to choose either to give up her children or become the second or third wife of an already married brother of her late husband. Remaining unmarried is almost impossible in

10 PRACTICAL ANTHROPOLOGY, March-April 1970, pp. 60—61.

traditional African society unless she wants to turn to prostitution.

Complicating Omodo's situation was the fact that his late brother's wife had become blind. There are no pensions for widows, no homes for the aged and blind in the traditional African society.

Therefore Omodo is right when he claims that marrying her was an act of unselfish mercy and when he observes with critical irony, "Actually my older brother would have been next in line. But he is a church elder and not allowed to sin by giving security to a widow." To marry a blind woman and accept the responsibility for her children was certainly a sacrifice.

However, I would have talked to her, too, and asked how she felt about her situation. I have seen courageous widows in Africa who have stayed alone and who have supported their children through their own hard work, without going into prostitution. But they were rare exceptions and they lived in an urbanized situation or were employed by the church or the mission. For a *blind* widow even this possibility is out.

If she wanted to stay with Omodo, I would not have demanded him, not even after his baptism, to divorce her — unless her congregation was prepared to take full responsibility for her and her children.

Would then the "walls break" and the church

be "flooded with polygamists"? I do not believe so, especially since polygamy is on the retreat in Africa anyway, mostly for economic reasons. Then too, the young generation of Africans look for a monogamous marriage of partnership. At least this "flooding" is not the experience of the Lutheran Church in Liberia. This church adopted the policy of baptizing polygamists in 1951. Dr. Roland Payne, the African President of the Church, reports that these cases have certainly been the exceptions.

If the motives are carefully discerned and the counseling approach dealing with each polygamist brother individually is used, there is no danger. This approach, however, would demand an army of trained counselors. In order to emphasize this, I would like my African co-worker, Jean Banyolak, to put it in his own words.

I will close this book with the sermon I preached at the marriage of Jean and Ernestine Banyolak in Europe. This sermon contains a direct answer for Omodo, who still lives in the "garden concept of marriage" as it is called in the sermon.

It brings forth the biblical meaning of monogamy. It is my deep conviction that the most urgent need today is not the negative approach of fighting against polygamy in Africa or the "sex morass" in the west, but rather the positive approach of interpreting what monogamy, lived in Jesus Christ, really means.

AFRICA NEEDS MARRIAGE COUNSELORS
by Jean Banyolak, Cameroun

Why are marriage counselors necessary at all? Haven't centuries passed during which people married and families lived without the aid of a marriage counselor?

Of course, there have always been marriage counselors, but in a different form. According to the custom of my village, after a quarrel between husband and wife, the wife leaves the house of her husband and returns to her parents. Then the husband follows her to her home village and the wife's family gives their judgment about the matter. In this family court the parents of the wife have the supreme authority. If the case is not very serious, they counsel the quarrelling couple and tell them how they should act from now on in order not to have palavers. In this case, we could say that the marriage counselors for this couple in difficulty are the members of the wife's family.

Or the young couple might live in the home of the husband's parents (though less often now than formerly). In this case, the husband's parents think they have the right to interfere in all the problems and decisions which the young couple have. Their parental counsel, based on their patriarchal authority, is often respected and acted upon. If, for example, the young wife makes a mistake, then the husband goes to his own mother and asks her to teach his wife how she should act toward him. The husband's mother then teaches the young wife how to please her husband so that all goes well. On the other hand, the husband's father counsels his son on how to treat a woman. In this second case, we see that the young couple's marriage counselors are the husband's parents.

In my country one could say that, generally speaking, the marriage counselor of the new generation is the older generation. Obviously this was taken for granted in former times. It was the natural thing because for hundreds of years the same rhythm of life was carried on without great changes. Thus, through experience the older generation knew exactly what to do in all domains of life.

However, since the beginning of the industrial revolution, the structure of the family has changed. The fathers of the family leave their homes early in the morning to go to work and are only at home during their hours of leisure. The children become independent at a very young age and live on their own salaries far from their families. The wives and mothers of the family are no longer content just to do their household tasks at home, but also look for a paying job.

The result is that many decisions, which were made formerly by the family as a whole or by the clan, are made today by the individual or the young couple. But they are not prepared to make them. They have no rules, no standards, no guide. The customs and traditions which formerly served as guides are not sufficient in this new situation. This is why the older generation feels itself incapable to guide the new.

It is no wonder then that one hears cries for help. The request for guidance by personal counsel becomes urgent. The marriage counselor becomes a necessity. This is true for all societies where the industrial revolution has already taken place. The many offices in America and in Europe, organized by the church and by the state, offering marriage guidance, are proof of this fact.

For us in Africa, the need for marriage guidance is perhaps even more important since the industrial revolution has advanced so rapidly.

The development which has taken place in western society over a period of centuries has taken place in Africa during a single generation or even in a decade. For this reason the problems of the individual and the couple are even more touchy; the conflict between that which is old and that which is new becomes even more intense and the confusion greater.

Therefore, Africa needs marriage counselors.

WEDDING SERMON FOR AN AFRICAN COUPLE
(preached to a European congregation)

Jean Banyolak, a teacher from Cameroun and former student of Pastor Trobisch, came to Germany in 1964 to receive an education as a marriage counsellor. In 1965, his fiancée, Ernestine Bout, followed him. The church wedding was celebrated on Easter Monday, 1965, at Gengenbach in the Black Forest, Germany, as a part of the morning worship service.

The following message is a translation of the wedding sermon preached in German by Pastor Trobisch who married the couple. The reader should not forget that the listeners to this sermon were almost exclusively Europeans. In an indirect way, this sermon answers also some of the questions which were left open by the case of Omodo.

Be subject to one another out of reverence for Christ. Wives, be subject to your husbands, as to the Lord. For the husband is the head of the wife as Christ is the head of the church, his body, and is himself its Saviour. As the church is subject to Christ, so let wives also be subject in everything to their husbands. Husbands, love your wives, as Christ loved the church and gave

*himself up for her, that he might sanctify her,
having cleansed her by the washing of water with
the word, that he might present the church to
himself in splendour, without spot or wrinkle or
any such thing, that she might be holy and without
blemish. Even so husbands should love their
wives as their own bodies. He who loves his wife
loves himself. For no man ever hates his own
flesh, but nourishes and cherishes it, as Christ
does the church, because we are members of his
body. "For this reason a man shall leave his father and mother and be joined to his wife, and
the two shall become one." This is a great mystery, and I take it to mean Christ and the church;
however, let each one of you love his wife as
himself, and let the wife see that she respects
her husband.* (Eph. 5 : 21-33)

This text contains one phrase to which all men
in the whole world would gladly agree: "Wives,
be subject to your husbands."

The reaction of an African husband is apt to
be something like this: "Wonderful! This is exactly what I think! Wives should be subject in
everything to their husbands. Did you hear? In
everything! I believe with all my heart that the
Bible is right. It confirms my conviction that men
are made to rule and women to obey. They are
inferior beings, belonging to the second class.
It's great that even God agrees with me!"

We find this discrimination against women not
only in Africa. It can be traced to almost all

cultures of the earth. It permeates the history of mankind. "Educate a woman and you put a knife into the hands of a monkey," the Brahmins said in India. Originally, the wedding ring which we wear today was in the Germanic culture a ring which the bride had around her neck. A chain was connected to it, and thus the husband, riding high on his horse, led his young wife home after the wedding ceremony. As late as 1897 the German theologian Bettex wrote: "Continuous activity of the brain nerves has a negative effect on the female organism. Therefore the hope that a woman can be educated scientifically and politically is utopian." Even today Europeans usually feel disappointed when "only" a girl is born.

Where does this downward outlook toward women come from? Is it because a man is stronger, more intelligent and resourceful? Or because he has seized the money and the power?

To me, only one explanation seems plausible. It is the explanation which Dr. and Mrs. David Mace offer in their book *Marriage East and West.* They say that the discrimination against women is due to a false biological concept of the process of procreation. Before science defeated this concept, it seemed obvious and logical.

The old concept of procreation was this: The husband is the bearer of the seed of life; the wife is the soil — the garden. Just as a plant grows out of a seed of grain, so does the child grow out of the man's seed. The body of the mother is just nourishing soil. But the man sows the seed and the substance of man grows into the child.

Most African languages use this vocabulary when describing the process of propagation. It was universal thinking until 1759 when the anatomist Kaspar Friedrich Wolff, in a thesis for his medical degree at Halle University, proved for the first time that both parents contribute something to the substance of the offspring. Not until 1944 was the union of the parent cells, sperm and egg, actually observed for the first time by the microscope.

This explains why the "garden concept of marriage", as I call it, could reign for such a long time. It is still prevalent in Africa. The ethical consequences of this false biological concept are tremendous.

First of all, the conclusion is that the child is the man's child. The woman simply carries his child. If the child is a son, it continues the man's life, living on in his family, thus giving the man's life meaning and purpose. Consequently sons are more appreciated than daughters. When one asks an African father how many children he has, he will very likely be told only the number of sons. When a European father states that he has three children, one may often discover that he actually has three daughters.

The next conclusion is this: Men are more important than women just as the bearer of the seed is more important than the soil. The woman's function is inferior to the man's function. By her very nature the woman is secondary and auxiliary. Perhaps this is the root of the discrimination between man and woman.

This garden concept is reflected in the African custom of bride-wealth. The man acquires for himself a garden — or rather what grows in the garden. The bride-wealth is a refund for the reproductive powers which the wife's clan loses. In other words, it is given for the children which the wife is going to bear. If she bears a child before the bride-wealth is given in full to her family, then this child, according to the rule of many African tribes, still belongs to her father and not yet to her husband, because her father is still the legal owner of the garden.

The garden concept also affects the choice of the marriage partner. Naturally a garden cannot make a choice. In the traditional society the girl had very little to say about the choice of her future husband. The father gave his garden to whom he desired, most likely to the one who offered the best exchange. The main criterion for the young suitor's choice was the fertility of the soil he was going to acquire. This is why, still today, virgins are usually preferred because it is believed that virgin soil is more productive.

Naturally in this garden concept a child constitutes the only purpose of marriage, if not of life. A childless marriage is meaningless. In this case there are two possibilities: successive or simultaneous polygamy. Either the husband divorces the wife — returns the garden to its owner and demands the refund of the bride-wealth in order to acquire another garden — or the husband adds a second garden along with the first and hopes that the second will bear fruit.

Polygamy is the logical result of the garden concept. It is a man's concept. A man can own several gardens. Each garden, however, can only belong to one man.

This is the situation we have to face now in Africa. I hope you can imagine to a small degree at least what it means to proclaim in Africa today a text like, "Therefore a man leaves his father and his mother and cleaves to his wife, and they become one flesh" (Gen. 2 : 24). Like a hammer crushing rocks, it defeats the garden concept in every single point.

Jean Banyolak, our bridegroom, was an upper classman at Cameroun Christian College, where we used Dr. Theodor Bovet's *A Handbook to Marriage*[11] as a text in our marriage class. In this book Dr. Bovet makes the following statement: "One of the most fundamental rules of married life is that husband and wife shall never again employ the expression 'my family' or 'your family'. These bonds should have been dissolved by the marriage, leaving only 'our family'".

In Europe I did not have any difficulty with these

11 Theodor Bovet, A HANDBOOK TO MARRIAGE (Doubleday, New York, 1958).

words. But when we read them in Cameroun, the students took offense. There was a real uproar in class. The wife should leave — that was understandable. In a patriarchal society, that goes without saying, just as it did in Israel. But that the *man* should leave? Leave his father instead of continuing his life? No! Never! This was unacceptable. The students interpreted this demand as an offense against their ancestors, as ungratefulness to those who had given them the gift of life.

And yet this word "leave" may be the most necessary word for Africa today. It may cause the one great basic revolution which is necessary in order to make all the small revolutions succeed. It may upset the whole economic system. If a man leaves his father and his mother — not leave them in the lurch, but leave them in order to establish his own home, his own family — instead of joining his family to the clan, he becomes economically independent. His economic resources can thus be used in the interest of the nation, instead of in the interest of his tribe. Therefore the word "leave" might reach deeply into politics.

Why are there so many difficulties in the young African states today? No longer is it white colonialist exploitation which hinders independence; it is the exploitation of the couple by the clan. Obedience to the commandment "leave!" may cause the downfall of tribalism, Africa's greatest enemy today. There can be no independent nations if there are no independent couples.

"And cleaves to his wife." This is the second blow to the garden concept. Again, the *man* cleaves to the wife, not the other way around only. The joining becomes mutual. And what is still just as important and revolutionary, a man cleaves to the *wife,* not to his clan. He gives his children to his wife, not to his clan. Being joined together, cleaving together, means that husband and wife become closest to each other, closer than to anyone else.

Within the garden concept a woman views herself as the daughter of her mother in the first place, as the mother of her children in the second place, and only in the third place as the wife of her husband. Husband and wife become parallel for the purpose of procreation, but they are not really united. The wife confides in her sisters, but not in her husband. The husband confides in his brothers, but not in his wife.

When I suggested to my African students that a husband should tell his wife how much money he earns, they hit the ceiling. Impossible, they said, how can you trust a woman? But do you know that eighty percent of German husbands do not tell their wives how much they earn either?

The marriage of trust and love will start another very necessary revolution in Africa. A man who marries a girl because he loves her is closer to her than to his clan. Therefore is a real war going on in Africa today — a war of the clan against the marriage of love. The clan is Africa's fetish. The marriage of love will overthrow this idol and overcome eventually the narrow-minded clan-egotism.

On the other hand, the marriage of love will create the nuclear families which alone are able to serve the extended family. It will prove that to leave the parents does not mean to abandon the parents. It will prove that a couple which has a chance to really *leave*, to exist independently without being indebted, will be able to really help their parents. The health of the extended family depends upon the health of the nuclear family. The marriage of love will change the extended family from a group which seeks its own interest to a group which contributes constructively to society as a whole.

Jean and Ernestine Banyolak, who sit here among us, have left their parents 4000 miles away. It is a tremendous step for an African couple to marry in a foreign country. But if they are getting married today because they love each other and intend to remain closest to each other — they start a revolution. Let us pray for them in this respect.

"And they become one flesh." One. Not parallel, but one! This is the third blow to the garden concept. They become united as one single body, one flesh. It is not the substance of the man which grows into the child as the garden concept concludes. The man and woman both contribute to the child. In stating that "they become one flesh" the Bible is scientifically correct — 3000 years before the microscope could establish this truth.

The child belongs to both of them. There is absolute equality. Both have to leave, both have to cleave. Both become one flesh.

However, such equality is possible only between two partners. Three can never become one, especially since the expression "one flesh" touches not only the physical realm, but also life as a whole. They are to share equally all that they are and have. The biblical concept of equality excludes polygamy.

It is not difficult to imagine that with this changed concept of marriage a great need arises in Africa today. Many Africans are saying: "We would like to have such a marriage. But how do we go about it? How does one live with an equal partner?" Many complain: "Our women are just not yet ready for this kind of equality."

In many cases they are right. Therefore let us pray for the bride in our midst — that she may become a real partner to her husband and that through her testimony she may become a contributor to the African society. There can be no doubt: The future of the African woman decides the future of the African continent.

But now comes the most surprising thing in our text — the final death blow to the garden concept. It is the period, the full stop after this verse 24. "And they become one flesh." Period. Full stop.

In this verse about marriage, quoted four times in the Bible, there is not one word about children.

There must be no misunderstanding: The Bible is not hostile to children. On the contrary, according to the Bible, children are a blessing of God. But they are an *additional* blessing of God.

The message of the period, of the full stop, is simply this: It is not the child which makes marriage, as marriage has meaning even when it is childless. That man and wife become "one flesh" is meaning enough. Children originate from the one-flesh union. But they do not constitute it. The fellowship of love between husband and wife is the fulfillment of marriage in itself.

The consequences of this full stop for Africa cannot be overemphasized. Its message is like a stick of dynamite thrown into African society. If the child is not the *only* meaning of marriage, the whole garden concept is blown up. It affects virtually all African marriage customs.

The bride-wealth system will lose its meaning, for it is a compensation for the fertile garden, not for the childless woman. Childlessness will no longer be a reason for divorce. Neither simultaneous nor successive polygamy can be justified any longer because of childlessness. The standards for the choice of a marriage partner will change from fertility to personality. The girl will be married for her own sake and not for what she is going to produce. This full stop, this period, makes out of the woman a human being.

But then our African brethren will ask: "What is the deepest meaning of marriage? If it means something more than just the production of children, what is it?"

There is only one answer to this question: It is the freely given mutual love between husband and wife. Thus far the church has confronted the African society with a negative message on marriage by saying: Those who have more than one wife cannot become church members. But it has failed to proclaim a positive message on marriage. It has failed to interpret to Africa the meaning of monogamous married love.

At this point, however, we stand with empty hands in front of our African friends. I was often ashamed in front of my former student, Jean Banyolak, when he came to Germany. What would he see when he was invited into our families? What would he witness when he went through the streets of our cities at night? What would he conclude when he went to a movie or read a magazine?

We Europeans are just as poor as the Africans when it comes to this positive testimony. The monogamous union of love is not a western concept. It is a divine concept. Therefore there is only one way to make clear to Africans and Europeans alike what married love really is. It is the way which the Apostle Paul chose when he wrote his letter to the Ephesians. He pointed to the love of the Son of God: "Husbands, love your wives, as Christ loved the church and gave himself up for her" (Eph. 5 : 25).

52

How did Christ love the church? He served her! He did not come to be served, but to serve. He lowered himself to become the lowliest servant, giving himself up for her when dying at the cross.

Now the circle closes. What then does it mean, "Wives, be subject to your husbands, as to the Lord?" The last four words make all the difference. It is not a forced submission to a superior ruler. According to the Bible this patriarchal subordination is a result of sin — "and he shall rule over you" (Gen. 3 : 16). "As to the Lord" is a different submission. It is a voluntary submission *in response* to the submission of her husband.

Why do we submit ourselves to Christ? Because he rules over us like a patriarch? No. We submit to him out of gratefulness, because he submitted himself to us first. We love him, because he loved us first. We serve him, because he served us first.

In the same way, a wife submits to her husband out of gratefulness because he submitted to her first. "Be subject to one another out of reverence for Christ."

In Christ, the wife becomes again the equal "helper fit for him" she was meant to be. In Christ, the husband becomes the equal helper fit for her that he was meant to be. In Christ, both become fully human. Their marriage will reflect the love of Jesus Christ. This mystery is great. It is the deepest meaning of married love.